Math Games and Activities with Dice

IPMG Publishing

Math Games and Activities with Dice

Copyright © 2010, IPMG Publishing

IPMG Publishing
18362 Erin Bay
Eden Prairie, Minnesota 55347

phone: (877) 702-6284

www.iplaymathgames.com

ISBN 978-1-934218-03-7

IPMG Publishing provides Mathematics Resource Books and Activity Books to companies, schools and individuals. The publisher of this book grants permission for the teacher or parent to reproduce recording sheets for classroom or personal use only. Any further duplication is prohibited.

All rights reserved. Printed in the United States of America.

Contents

Introduction		2
Around the Schoolyard	(Grades 4-7)	4
Countdown	(Grades 3-5)	7
Cover Up	(Grades 1-5)	8
Lucky Number	(Grades 2-4)	10
Magnificent Flying Machines	(Grades K-2)	13
Making Connections	(Grades 4-6)	14
Math Baseball	(Grades 3-6)	16
Over The Edge	(Grades 2-3)	20
Save The Ducklings	(Grades 2-3)	21
Snake Eyes	(Grades 1-4)	22
Shake 'Em Up	(Grades 1-3)	24
Top It Off	(Grades 2-3)	26
Woodchuck!	(Grades 1-3)	28
0 to 99	(Grades 1-3)	30
Decimal Dice	(Grades 2-4)	31
Fraction Dice Bingo	(Grades 3-5)	33
Fraction Dice Race	(Grades 3-6)	35
Pass It On	(Grades 4-6)	38
Pizza Fractions Game	(Grades 3-4)	39
Your Number's Up	(Grades 2-3)	41
Dice Tic Tac Toe	(Grades 6-8)	43
Power Play	(Grades 6-8)	44
Block Builder	(Grades 1-3)	45
Name That Number, Fraction or Shape	(Grades 2-6)	46
One Meter Dash	(Grades 1-3)	51
It's Your Call	(Grades 1-2)	52
654	(Grades 4-6)	54
3 Ways to Win	(Grades 5-7)	55
Two Dice Sums	(Grades 5-7)	57
Dice Calendar Puzzle	(Grades 4-6)	59
Stacking Dice Puzzles	(Grades 3-5)	60
Touching Faces Dice Puzzles	(Grades 3-5)	62
Rolling 3 Dice Trick	(Grades 7-8)	64
Touching Faces Dice Trick	(Grades 7-8)	65
Standard Cube Template		66
Octahedral Dice Template		67
Dodecahedron Dice Template		68
Selected Answers and Comments		69

Introduction

Dice have been used as a recreational pastime for thousands of years. One of the earliest examples is the four-sided dice from Egyptian tombs. Etruscan dice, found near Rome, and made about 900 B.C.E., are similar to the dice of today.

During the 12th and 13th centuries, dice spread throughout England and were often played by men in taverns for almost anything, even their clothing.

Because of the link to gambling, dice games met with strong disapproval by many of the early colonists in America. Despite these admonitions, dice still became a common household item in the North American colonies and have remained a part of the standard gaming inventory in most homes ever since.

Many dice games have been passed down through the centuries. A few of the games have even been modified and marketed by commercial vendors. Unfortunately, few resources are available to provide a link between this powerful motivational tool and mathematics instruction in Grades 2-8. That is the purpose of this resource book. It is our hope that you and your students will not only be able to relive the excitement of playing dice games, but that they will also sharpen their math skills. The games and activities usually stimulate a discussion as a follow up to each session. These discussions are important because they enhance students' vocabulary development, speaking skills, links to the math content and provide opportunities to suggest improvements to a game or to design a new game. Most of the material can be copied and used immediately. Some games are generic in nature and designed to be modified by teachers and/or students. The games and activities are also useful ideas to send home to families or as summer fun. If some parents are concerned about the potential link to gambling, encourage them to refer to the dice as number cubes.

The table of contents groups the games and activities by topic. Within each topic the games are organized alphabetically, but not sequentially. Teacher comments and selected answers are also provided.

Why use dice?

Dice are:
A useful diagnostic tool
Highly motivating
Flexible! They can be used at numerous grade levels and in many settings
Inexpensive and readily available
A powerful springboard to new topics based on pupil experience
Helpful as an aid to reinforce concepts
Effective as a tool to provide skill maintenance
A familiar, tactile, visual, yet mysterious and magical way to provide variety

When and where to use dice:

As a class starter.
Friday afternoon.
Special days and events.
Day before holiday.
As a "sponge" or "filler."
Whenever the objective warrants.
Individually.
One on one.
In small groups.
As an entire class.
As an activity station.

Management tips for using dice games:

Make sure the game fits your objectives.
Explain the rules before play using transparent dice or "giant" dice.
Establish ground rules before play begins.
Keep the group size at four or less.
Match students of comparable ability in competitive games.
Be sure to provide a follow up discussion for each game. The discussion can include sharing strategies to win, questions and what was learned from the game.
If parents are concerned about the link to gambling, send a sample game home with a note explaining the objective of the game.
Use the games sparingly.

Materials

Three customized dice labeled as shown below for each group.

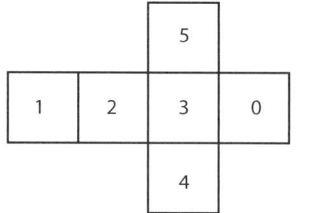

One *Around the Schoolyard* game board for each player/team.
One place marker for each player/team.

Rules and Play

1. This is a division of whole numbers with remainders dice game for 2-4 players/teams. The object of the game is to be the first player/team to go all around the schoolyard by solving problems. Players must travel from start to finish, counterclockwise, one station at a time.

2. To start the game, each player/team places a place marker at the start. Next, the first player/team rolls all three dice. In every dice roll, three 1-digit numbers will appear. The player/team must then select one number to be the divisor. The remaining numbers are used to form the dividend. For example, if the numbers were 8, 3, and 1, they could be arranged to form 18/3. If the quotient (6) is found in the next area of the schoolyard, the player/team advances the place marker.

3. Players/teams continue taking turns. Each problem must be in the form AB/C. Zero must not be used as the divisor, and only the numbers on the dice are to be used to obtain an answer.

4. The player/team that circles the schoolyard first wins.

Variations

- Change the numbers on the dice and playing board using the generic *Around the Schoolyard* game board master.

- Adapt the game to addition, subtraction, and multiplication by using two customized dice and the generic *Around the Schoolyard* game board.

- Redesign the game board to an interdisciplinary setting such as *Tour The Planets*.

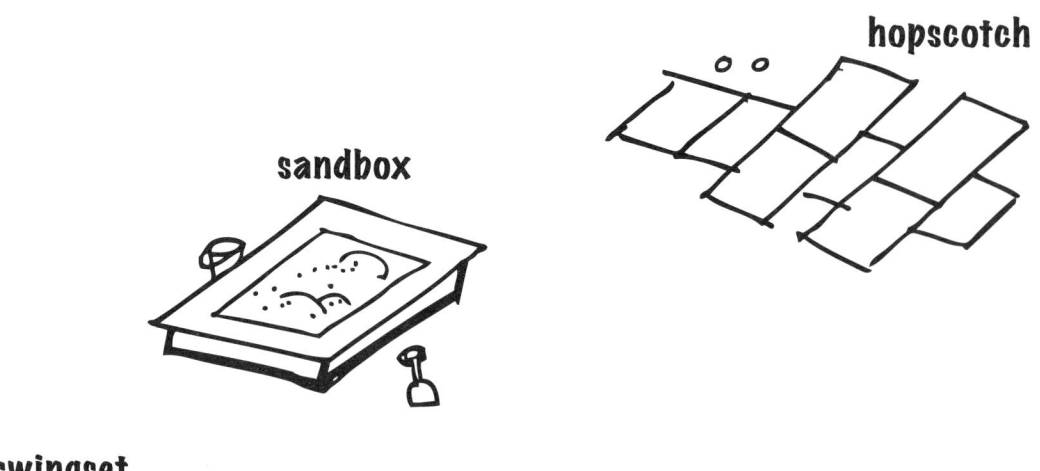

COUNT-DOWN

Materials

Two dice.

Rules and Play

1. This is a subtraction of whole numbers game for 2-4 players/teams. The object of the game is to be the first player/team to reach or go below zero.

2. Each player/team starts the game with 99 points (or whatever number desired). Players/teams take turns rolling the dice, finding the dice sums, and then subtracting the total from their score. After computing the results, the score is recorded and the dice pass to the next player/team.

3. Play continues until one player/team reaches or goes below zero.

Variations

- Change the goal so that the object is to come as close to zero as possible without going below it. A player/team who goes below zero is out of the game.

- For young students, use one die. Start at 29 so that the first roll does not require regrouping.

- Use other dice patterns or customized dice.

- Use any starting and stopping point. For example, start at 999 and stop at 700.

- Play using a calculator.

- To make the game more challenging, require players to finish exactly at zero.

- Use each die to represent a place value location. For example, if two dice were used and a 5 and a 7 were tossed, a player could subtract 57 or 75 from his/her score.

- Vary the number of dice. For example, use 3 dice, one die for ones, one die for tens, and one die for hundreds. Start the game at 2999.

- Adjust the numerals on the dice to include decimals, fractions, or integers.

- Limit the number of turns for a game. For example, the player/team closest to zero after 7 tries is the winner.

COVER UP

Materials

One playing board for each pair of players.
Two standard dice and counters for each pair of players.

Rules and Play

1. This is a dice game for 2 players.

2. Players sit on opposite side of the playing board. The *Cover Up* game board consists of two rows of numbered squares. Players take turns rolling the dice and adding the two numbers that appear. If the answer is correct, the square with the answer on the player's side of the board is covered. If a square is already covered, or an incorrect answer is given, the player must pass. The winner is the player with the greatest number of covered squares at the end of 10 rounds. If those numbers are the same, the game is tied. The time limit for each problem is 30 seconds.

Free	12	11	10	9	8	7	6	5	4	3	2

COVER UP GAME BOARD

2	3	4	5	6	7	8	9	10	11	12	Free

Variations

- Use more than two standard dice.

- Use different sets of whole numbers.

- Design a playing board for other operations like subtraction or multiplication.

COVER UP

Variations

Use blank *Cover Up* game boards to create your own game.

lucky number

Materials

One *Lucky Number* playing board.
One standard die.
One place marker for each player/team.

Rules and Play

1. This is a dice game for 1-5 players/teams.

2. The object of the game is to be the first player/team to travel from Start to Finish on the game board. When there is only one player or team, try to complete the course in as few turns as possible.

3. To begin the game, players must decide if they want to count up or down, and identify the starting number and increment. The first 3 entries are then recorded on the game board and the game begins. Players/teams take turns rolling the die and moving their counter the appropriate number of spaces. In order to stay at a new location, the player must identify the number based on the number pattern. For example, if a player rolled a 4 on his first turn, in a game involving skip counting by two's, beginning with 2, then (s)he would say 8. If an answer is incorrect, players must remain at their current location. Only one place marker may occupy a square. If two players or teams land on the same square, the last one stays and the other one must return to the Start position.

Variations

- Use more than one standard die.

- Use a customized die, labeled 0, 1, 2, 3, 4, 5, or some other convenient scheme.

- Use different sets of fractions, decimals, or integers to create a customized board like the examples shown below.

Positive and Negative Decimal Numbers

Count Up	Count Down
Starting Number: 1.99 (.001 to 99.9)	Starting Number: 1.5
Skip Counting Number: .01 (3 characters, 2 decimal places, .01 to 100)	Skip Counting Number: -.5 (3 characters, 2 decimal places, .01 to 100)
First Three Entries: 1.99, 2, 2.01	First Three Entries: 1.5, 1, .5

- Use an alternate rating scale for games involving one player or team.

Start   **lucky number**   Finish

Game Board

☐ Count Up

☐ Count Down

Skip Count By ___

Starting Number ___

Math Games and Activities with Dice
© IPMG Publishing

11

Record Sheet

Players/Teams

1 _____
2 _____
3 _____
4 _____
5 _____

Number of Turns	Rating
6	Lucky & Skillful!
7-10	Amazing!
11-14	Average
15-20	Unfortunate
21 or more	Unlucky

Game	Winner*	Rating**
1		
2		
3		
4		
5		

* Used only for games involving 2-5 players/teams
** Used only for games involving 1 player

Players/Teams

1 _____
2 _____
3 _____
4 _____
5 _____

Number of Turns	Rating
6	Lucky & Skillful!
7-10	Amazing!
11-14	Average
15-20	Unfortunate
21 or more	Unlucky

Game	Winner*	Rating**
1		
2		
3		
4		
5		

* Used only for games involving 2-5 players/teams
** Used only for games involving 1 player

Magnificent Flying Machines

Materials

Two standard dice for each player/team.
Paper and pencil for each player/team.

Instructions

1. This is a number recognition game for 2-4 players/teams. The object of the game is to be the first player/team to build a butterfly. The parts of the butterfly are the head, the body, wings, a face and two antennae.

2. At the start of the game, each player/team selects a number from 1-6 and writes it at the top of their Record Sheet. Next players/teams take turns rolling the dice. If a player/team rolls their number, they may draw one part of the butterfly. If a player/team rolls a double of their number, two butterfly parts can be drawn.

3. The first player/team to complete a butterfly wins.

Variations

- Change the rules so that a player must roll a 1 to draw the body, 2 to draw the head, 3 to draw the left antenna, 4 to draw the right antenna, 5 to draw the left wing, and 6 to draw the right wing.

- To make the game more challenging, change the butterfly construction so that player/team must first obtain a body and a head before adding wings and antennae.

- For subtraction facts practice, use two standard dice, roll the dice and find the difference. If the answer is 0, draw the body, 1 draw the head, 2 draw the left antenna, 3 draw the right antenna, 4 draw the left wing, 5 draw the right wing.

Making Connections

Materials

Four standard dice.
One *Making Connections* game board.
Four place markers for each player.

Rules and Play

1. This is a game for 2-3 players.

2. The object of the game is to be the first player to get four adjacent place markers in a row, column, or diagonal on the *Making Connections* board.

3. Play begins by rolling all 4 dice. The player who has rolled the dice then attempts to combine the numbers that are shown so that the final result is on the game board. The numbers on the dice may be arranged in any order using addition, subtraction, multiplication, or division. The maximum time limit for each play is one minute. If a player does not give an answer that is on the game board, (s)he loses a turn.

4. Once a player has an answer that is on the game board, (s)he places a place marker in the square. Play then passes to the next player.

5. A player may attempt to occupy any empty square. Only one place marker may occupy a square. Players must explain how the numbers they roll can be combined so that the answer is the number in the square they select. For example, if a player rolls a 6, 6, 4, and 5, (s)he could place a place marker on the square labeled 37, if it was not occupied, and if (s)he explained that
(6x6) + (5-4) = 37.

Variations

- On the first game, have players work on their own game boards. On subsequent games have players work on the same board so that blocking can occur.

- Allow the use of powers and square roots.

- Allow players to use calculators.

- Conduct a *Making Connections* tournament.

1	2	3	4	5	6	7	8
9	10	11	12	13	14	15	16
17	18	19	20	21	22	23	24
25	26	27	28	29	30	31	32
33	34	35	36	37	38	39	40
41	42	44	45	48	50	54	55
60	64	66	72	75	80	90	96
100	108	120	125	144	150	180	216

MATH BASEBALL

Materials

Two dice labeled 4-9 and four place markers.

Rules and Play

1. *Math Baseball* is a game for 1 or 2 players/teams.

2. Determine team names and who bats first by rolling the dice. Highest total bats last.

3. Roll the dice and multiply the two numbers shown on the dice. Players must give a correct answer to the problem posed by the dice and then locate the meaning of the answer on the "Hitting Chart." Use place markers to help remember who is on base.

4. Each player is given 3 outs per inning. An incorrect answer is an automatic out.

5. The player/team with the highest score after 5 innings is the winner.

Hitting Chart:
72-81   Home Run
71-66   Triple
65-51   Double
50-35   Single
16-35   Out

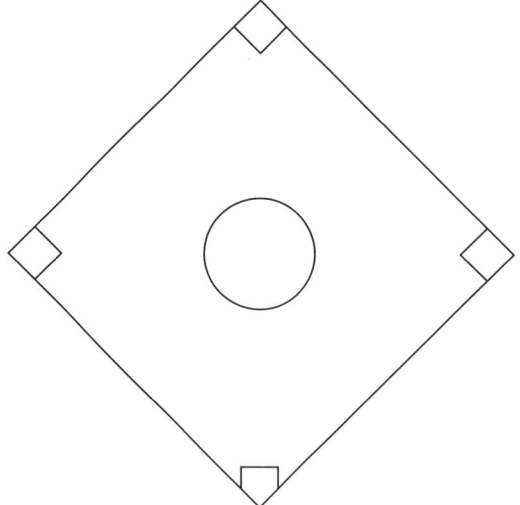

Team	Inning Score					Final

Variations

Sample custom made dice and hitting charts for addition, subtraction and division facts practice

Addition: First die, numbers 0-9. Second die, numbers 0-9.
Hitting Chart:
17-18   Home Run
15-16   Triple
12-14   Double
9-11   Single
0-8   Out

Subtraction: First die, numbers 10-19. Second die, numbers 0-9.
Hitting Chart:
18-19   Home Run
16-17   Triple
13-15   Double
10-12   Single
0-9   Out

Division: First die (divisors), numbers 1, 2, 3, 4, 5, 6. Second die (dividends), numbers 12, 14, 15, 20, 30, 42. (Note: Players roll until they have an integer result and then use the chart)
Hitting Chart:
21-42   Home Run
15-20   Triple
11-14   Double
6-10   Single
0-5   Out

MATH BASEBALL

Sample custom made dice and hitting charts for addition, subtraction, multiplication and division of decimals practice.

Addition of Decimals:
First die, numbers $.59, $.99, $1.59, $3.29, $.89, $1.75.
Second die, numbers $1.99, $.50, $.79, $2.98, $1.50, $2.49.

    Hitting Chart:
    $5 - $7   Home Run
    $4.26 - $4.99   Triple
    $3.51 - $4.25   Double
    $2.51 - $3.50   Single
    $1 - $2.50   Out

Subtraction of Decimals:
First die, numbers $10.00, $20.00, $20, $50, $100, $5.
Second die, numbers $2.95, $1.98, $4.99, $.97, $2.89, $3.50.

    Hitting Chart:
    $97.1 - $100   Home Run
    $50.10 - $97.50 Triple
    $45 - $50   Double
    $7 - $44.90   Single
    $0 - $6.99   Out

Multiplication of Decimals:
First die, numbers $150, $5, $25, $20, $10, $50.
Second die, numbers .1, .01, .05, .5, .25, .15.

    Hitting Chart:
    $25 - $80   Home Run
    $5 - $24   Triple
    $1 - $4   Double
    $.06 - $.9   Single
    $0 - $.05   Out

Division of Decimals:
First die (divisors), numbers .1, .01, .001, .5, .25, .0001.
Second die (dividends), numbers $150, $5, $25, $20, $10, $50.

    Hitting Chart:
    $250,000 - $1,500,000 Home Run
    $100,000 - $249,999   Triple
    $5001 - $99,999   Double
    $250 - $5000   Single
    $0 - $249   Out

Sample custom made dice and hitting charts for evaluating expressions practice.

Evaluating Expressions: $x^3 + 5$
Single die, labeled 0, 1, 2, 3, 4, 5.
For example, if a 3 is rolled and the expression is evaluated, 32 is the result.

Hitting Chart:
130   Home Run
69   Triple
32   Double
13   Single
5-6   Out

Evaluating Expressions: $x^y + 5$
Die x labeled 0, 1, 2, 3, 4, 5.
Die y labeled 1, 2, 3, 4, 5, 6.

Hitting Chart:
\> 1000   Home Run
251 - 1000   Triple
61 - 250   Double
7 - 60   Single
5 - 10   Out

Over the Edge

Materials

One standard die.
One *Over the Edge* record sheet.

Instructions

1. This is an addition and subtraction of whole numbers game for 2-4 players or teams. The object of the game is to come closest to the goal without going over.

2. Each player/team begins a game with a score of zero. Players/teams take turns rolling the die or dice. After each roll, players/teams add the value of the toss to their previous score. After computing the result, the score is recorded and the die pass to the next player/team. If a player/team running score exceeds the goal (30), they are out of the game.

3. The player/team closest to 30 at the end of each round of eight turns wins. If there is a tie, each player/team receives one point. The first player/team to score 3 points wins the game.

Round	Score	Running Total
1		
2		
3		
4		
5		
6		
7		
8		
	Final Score	

Variations

- Use two standard dice, or one or two customized dice.

- Change the goal. For example, 129, 99, or 59, etc.

- Start at 30, 99, etc. and finish at zero using 1, or 2 dice and subtraction.

Save the Ducklings

Materials

Two standard dice.
11" x 17" paper and pencil.
30 counters for each player.

Instructions

1. This is a counting, addition, and strategy game for 2-4 players or teams. The object of the game is to save the most ducklings by collecting the most counters.

2. At the start of the game, players draw a larger picture of the duck and trap on a sheet of paper (see below) and place it in the middle of the players.

3. Each player begins the game with 30 counters and rolls the dice in turn. Each counter represents one duckling. After rolling the dice, the player totals the dice values and places that number of counters on the matching section of the trap. If that section already contains counters, the player may take those counters and roll the dice again until the player rolls a total that corresponds to an empty section and loses counters.

4. Section 7 is known as the solitary cell section. In section 7 counters are collected, but not released. Each time a player rolls a 7 (s)he must add 7 counters to the center cell and must not remove any. It is then the next player's turn.

5. If a players rolls a total of 2 or 12, (s)he may collect all of the counters in the trap, including those in section 7. When a 2 or 12 is rolled, players also receive another turn. If a player rolls a 2 or 12 on his/her second turn, (s)he must place counters in each cell that corresponds to the number value of that cell of the trap (77 in all).

6. If a player loses all his/her counters, (s)he must drop out of the game.

7. Play continues until time is called, or only one player remains. The player who has saved the most ducklings wins.

Variations

- Change the rules so that each game ends after a predetermined number of rounds. The player with the high score at the end of X rounds wins.

Snake Eyes

Materials

Two ordinary dice for each player/team.
One *Snake Eyes* record sheet for each player/team.

Rules and Play

1. This is a game for 2-4 players/teams. The object of the game is to get the lowest score.

2. Players/teams take turns. After each roll players/teams eliminate any die that shows a one. Players/teams continue rolling the die or dice until both dice are eliminated. Players/teams count and record the number of rolls required to complete the task.

3. The player/team that requires the fewest number of rolls to eliminate both dice wins.

Variation

- Modify the game so that it is played with 3, 4, 5, 6, or 12 dice.

Questions

What is the minimum number of rolls required to eliminate both dice?

What is the average number of rolls needed to win?

What is the expected number of rolls needed to eliminate both dice?

Suppose you had to modify this game so that it could be used in as a gambling game for one person in a casino. If you worked for the casino, what payoff scheme would you recommend to your boss?

Project

Write a calculator program to simulate the *Snake Eyes* game. Allow a user to select from 2-12 dice in the game.

Math Games and Activities with Dice
© IPMG Publishing

Player 1			Player 2		
Round	Dice Eliminated	Dice Remaining	Round	Dice Eliminated	Dice Remaining
1			1		
2			2		
3			3		
4			4		
5			5		
6			6		
7			7		
8			8		
9			9		
10			10		
11			11		
12			12		
13			13		
14			14		
15			15		
16			16		
17			17		
18			18		
19			19		
20			20		
21			21		
22			22		
23			23		
24			24		
25			25		
26			26		
27			27		
28			28		
29			29		
30			30		

Materials

Five standard dice.
One *Shake 'em Up* record sheet.
One calculator (optional).

Directions

1. This is a dice game for 1-4 players or teams. The object of the game is to earn the highest score.

2. Players/teams take turns rolling the dice. After each roll, players/teams, add the values shown on the dice and record the score on a record sheet, using the table on the following page as a guide.

3. Play continues for 10 rounds or until time is called. The player/team with the high total wins.

Variations

- Change the goal. For example: Low score wins. The first player/team to reach 250 wins.

- Change the point values assigned to each total of the dice.

Record Sheet

Players/Teams

1 _____
2 _____
3 _____
4 _____

Round	Player 1	Player 2	Player 3	Player 4
1				
2				
3				
4				
5				
6				
7				
8				
9				
10				

Final Score				

Winner! _____

Materials

Two dice. The dice may be standard or custom made (an example shown below).
Instead of manufacturing custom dice, use sticker labels to cover the dots and write in your own values.
One *Top It Off* record sheet.

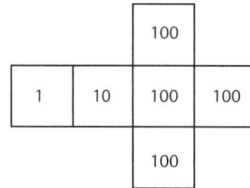 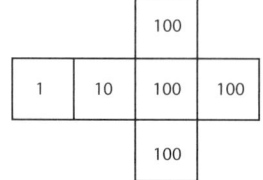

Rules and Play

1. This is a place value and addition of whole numbers game for 2-3 players/teams. The object of the game is to be the first player/team to reach or go above 2000.

2. Each player/team starts the game with 200 (or whatever number desired). Players/teams take turns rolling the dice, finding the dice sum and then adding the result to their score. Players/teams must record their dice total on their section of the score sheet and find their new running score.

3. Play continues until one player/team reaches or goes above 2000. An example of a game in progress is shown below.

Starting Number	Player 1	Player 2	Player 3
200	+101 = 301	+20 = 220	+110 = 310
	+110 = 411	+11 = 231	+20 = 330
	+200 = 611	+ =	+ =
	+ =	+ =	+ =

Variations

- Use place value mats and base 10 materials. Have students build collections directly on their place value mats.

- To make the game more challenging, require players to finish exactly at 2000.

- Use any starting and stopping point. For example, start at 700 and stop at 2500.

- Change the numbers on the dice.

Math Games and Activities with Dice
© IPMG Publishing

Record Sheet

Starting Number	Player 1	Player 2	Player 3
	+	+	+
	+	+	+
	+	+	+
	+	+	+
	+	+	+
	+	+	+
	+	+	+
	+	+	+
	+	+	+
	+	+	+
	+	+	+
	+	+	+
	+	+	+
	+	+	+
	+	+	+
	+	+	+
	+	+	+
	+	+	+

Wood Chuck!

Materials

Two customized dice.
One *Woodchuck!* record sheet.

Rules and Play

1. This is a dice game for 1-4 players.

2. Each die has five numbers, with a woodchuck on the sixth face. Each player may roll the dice as long as (s)he answers correctly. Each correct answer is added to the player's score for that round. If one woodchuck is rolled, or a problem is answered incorrectly, the player loses a turn and the score for that round. If the player elects to pass after points have been earned for that turn, the score for that round is added to player's total. If two woodchucks are rolled during a player's turn, points for that round and the total score are lost. Examples are shown below.

    Addition: First die, 5 numbers 0-9 and a woodchuck. Second die, 5 numbers 0-9 and a woodchuck. Goal: 90.

    Subtraction: First die, 5 numbers 0-9 and a woodchuck. Second die, 5 numbers 0-9 and a woodchuck. Goal 90.

    Multiplication: First die, numbers 2, 3, 4, 5, 6 and a woodchuck. Second die, numbers 10, 20, 40, 50, 100 and a woodchuck. Goal: 6000.

    Division: First die, divisors 3, 9 and a woodchuck. Second die, dividends 9, 18, 36, 54, 45, 27 and a woodchuck. Goal: 180.

3. Players may roll or pass on each turn.

4. The winner is the first player to reach the goal.

Variations

- For young children, use only one die, addition and a goal of 40.

- To make the game more challenging, change the dice and the goal so that the game is played with larger whole numbers, decimals, or fractions. In general, to estimate a reasonable goal for a game, find the largest difference between values on the two dice and multiply by 10.

Game 1

Operation:
Goal:

Round	Running Total
1	
2	
3	
4	

Game 2

Operation:
Goal:

Round	Running Total
1	
2	
3	
4	

Game 3

Operation:
Goal:

Round	Running Total
1	
2	
3	
4	

Game 4

Operation:
Goal:

Round	Running Total
1	
2	
3	
4	

Game 5

Operation:
Goal:

Round	Running Total
1	
2	
3	
4	

Game 6

Operation:
Goal:

Round	Running Total
1	
2	
3	
4	

0 to 99

Materials

Two standard dice.

Rules and Play

1. This is a mental arithmetic game involving addition and subtraction of whole numbers for 2-6 players/teams. The object is to be the last player in the game by forcing opponents to roll a value which makes the running total larger than 99.

2. Each game starts with a running total of zero.

3. Play proceeds clockwise around the playing area. In turn, each player tosses the dice and finds the sum. If the sum is any number except 9 or 10, the sum is added to the running total. If the sum is 9 or 10, then the player has the option to add or subtract the sum from the running total. Each player must roll on each turn and state the new correct running total. If a player's answer is incorrect, that player loses a turn. An example of a game in progress is shown below.

    The previous running total is 80. Player 1 rolls 3, 4 and announces that the new running total is 87. Player 2 rolls 6, 6 and announces that the new running total is 99. Player 3 rolls 5, 4 and announces that the new running total is 90.

4. The winner is the last player not having to state a running total larger than 99.

Variations

- Use a different goal and starting value. For example, start at 1895 and stop at 2000.

- Use other dice patterns.

- Use customized dice and allow calculator use.

Decimal Dice

Materials

One or two custom dice as shown below.
One *Decimal Dice* game board for each player/team.

Rules and Play

1. This is a game for 2-4 players/teams. The object of the game is to be the first player to completely cover his/her game board.

2. Players take turns rolling the dice. If the objective of the game is decimal sums, the player would find the sum of the two decimals shown on the dice and then locate the result on the game board. If this spot is vacant, he/she covers it and then passes the dice to next player. If the spot has already been covered, he/she must also pass the dice to the next player.

3. The first player to cover all 9 squares on the board is the winner. Sample dice patterns and game boards for 2 different games are shown below.

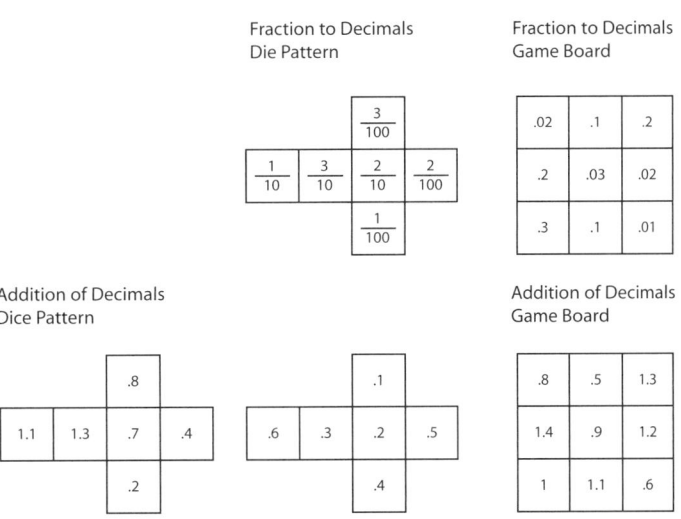

Variation

- To provide practice with addition, subtraction, multiplication, and division of whole numbers, percent, or a variety of other topics, such as exponents and scientific notation, simply adjust the dice and the game board to suit the need of the group. As the complexity of the exercises increases, some consideration may need to be given to providing players with calculators. If short games are desired, change the rules so that any set of 3 marks in a row, column, or diagonal wins. Additional ways to vary this game include expanding the board and using dice that are not cubes.

Decimal Dice

Decimal Dice

Decimal Dice

Decimal Dice

Decimal Dice

Fraction Dice Bingo

Materials

Four custom dice. Two cubes labeled 1- 6, and two labeled 5- 10.
One *Fraction Dice Bingo* Card for each player/team.
About 20 counters for each player/team.

Rules and Play

1. This is an equivalent fractions and mixed numbers dice game for 2-4 players. The object of the game is to be the first player to get five counters in a row, column or diagonal on their card.

2. To start the game, each player creates his/her own card using 25 numbers from the set below.

$$1, 1\tfrac{1}{2}, 1\tfrac{1}{3}, 1\tfrac{1}{4}, 1\tfrac{1}{5}, 1\tfrac{1}{6}, 1\tfrac{1}{7}, 1\tfrac{1}{8}, 1\tfrac{1}{9}, 1\tfrac{1}{10}, 1\tfrac{3}{4}, 1\tfrac{2}{3}, 1\tfrac{2}{7}, 1\tfrac{3}{7}, 1\tfrac{1}{2}, 1\tfrac{2}{5}, 1\tfrac{3}{5}, 1\tfrac{4}{5},$$
$$2, 2\tfrac{1}{2}, 2\tfrac{1}{3}, 2\tfrac{1}{4}, 2\tfrac{2}{3}, 3, 3\tfrac{1}{2}, 3\tfrac{1}{3}, 3\tfrac{1}{4}, 4, 4\tfrac{1}{2}, 5, 6, 7, 8, 9, 10$$

3. Players take turns rolling any two cubes and using the numbers rolled to make an improper fraction. After an improper fraction is made, players cover the equivalent number or mixed number with a counter.

4. The player that covers 5 squares in a row, column, or diagonal first wins.

Variations

- Change the pattern needed to win. For example, cover all, 4 corners + center, the letter X, with the letter C, the letter I, etc.

- For a more challenging game, have players create their cards form this set of numbers:

$$\tfrac{1}{2}, \tfrac{1}{3}, \tfrac{1}{4}, \tfrac{1}{5}, \tfrac{1}{8}, \tfrac{3}{4}, \tfrac{3}{8}, \tfrac{1}{2}, \tfrac{5}{8}, \tfrac{3}{4} \qquad \tfrac{1}{7}, \tfrac{2}{7}, \tfrac{3}{7}, \tfrac{4}{7}, \tfrac{5}{7}, \tfrac{6}{7}$$

$$1\tfrac{1}{6}, 1\tfrac{1}{7}, 1\tfrac{1}{8}, 1\tfrac{1}{9}, 1\tfrac{1}{2}, 1\tfrac{1}{4}, 2, 2\tfrac{1}{4}, 2\tfrac{3}{4} \qquad \tfrac{1}{9}, \tfrac{2}{9}, \tfrac{4}{9}, \tfrac{5}{9}, \tfrac{7}{9}, \tfrac{8}{9}$$

$$1\tfrac{2}{3}, 2\tfrac{1}{3}, 2\tfrac{2}{3}, 3\tfrac{1}{3}, 1, 1\tfrac{1}{5}, 1\tfrac{2}{5}, 1\tfrac{3}{5}, 1\tfrac{4}{5} \qquad 1\tfrac{1}{3}, 1\tfrac{1}{6}, 1\tfrac{2}{3}, 1\tfrac{5}{6}, 2\tfrac{1}{2}, 3, 4, 4\tfrac{1}{2}, 5, 6, 7$$

Fraction Dice Bingo

Materials

One to three customized dice.
One *Fraction Dice Race* game board.
One place marker for each player.

Directions

1. *Fraction Dice Race* is a game for 2-3 players. The object of the game is to be the first player to travel from start to finish on the *Fraction Dice Race* game board on the following page.

2. To begin the game, all players place their marker on start. Players take turns rolling the die or dice. In a one die game, players move the fraction of a space indicated on the die. In a two dice game, players add or subtract the numbers shown and then move the resulting fraction of a unit. For example, if a player rolls 1/3 + 1/3 then (s)he must move forward 2/3 of a unit. Players must read and obey any instructions that apply to the location or square they occupy. For example, if a player landed on the space with the instruction "Move to Happy Face", then (s)he must move to that square. Several players may occupy the same square.

3. The first player to reach the end of the track is the winner. Sample dice patterns and game boards for 2 different games are shown below.

One Die Fractions Pattern

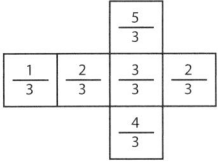

Addition and Subtraction of Fractions Dice

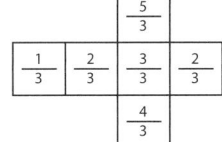 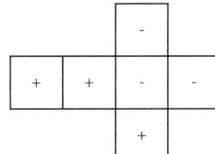

Variations

- Create a game board and dice for a game involving fourths, or some other fractional unit. Use the game boards on the following pages.

- Adjust the operation die so that only addition, or only subtraction symbols are provided.

- Change the fraction die or dice so that mixed numbers are used.

Math Games and Activities with Dice
© IPMG Publishing

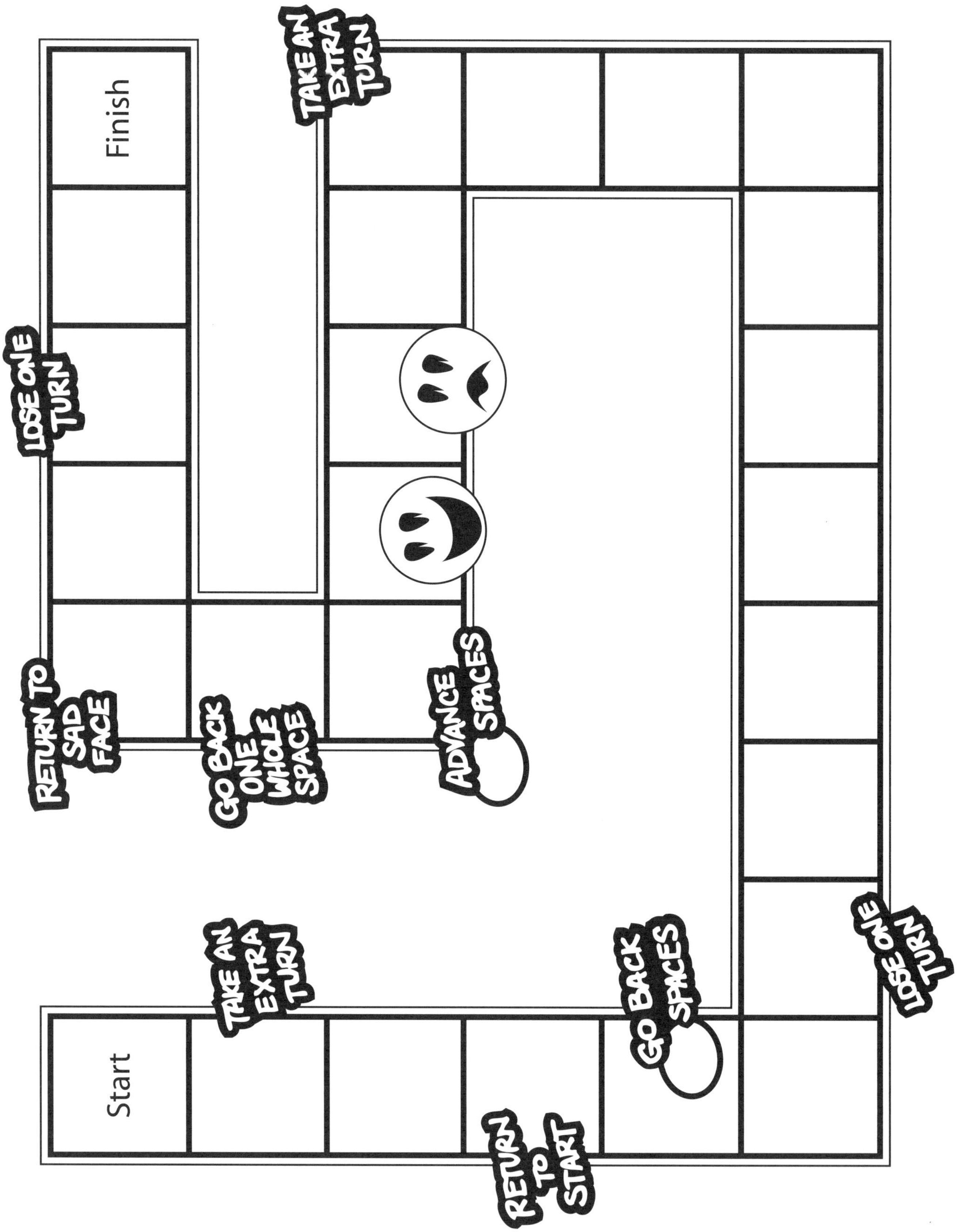

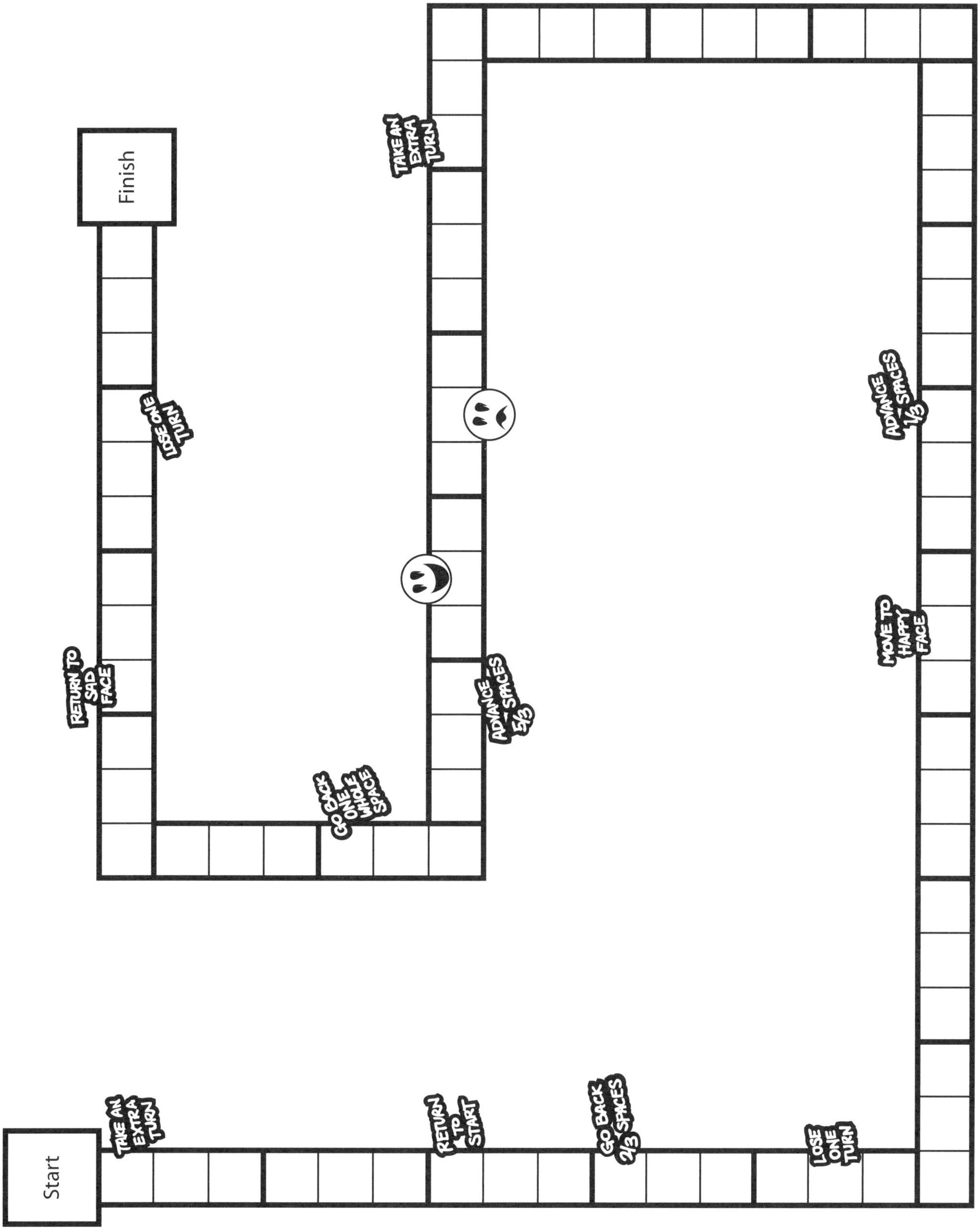

Pass It On

Materials

Five standard dice.
One cup.
Five playing chips for each player.

Rules and Play

1. This is a percent of a number game for 3-5 players. The youngest player starts first.

2. The object of the game is to collect the most chips.

3. Play begins by rolling all 5 dice. For each die, if the result is:

    6, put a chip in the cup.
    5, pass one chip to the player on your left.
    4, pass one chip to the player on your right.
    1, 2, or 3, do not pass any chips or put any in the cup.

4. If the number of chips in your possession is less than 5, you only roll that number of dice. For example, if you had 3 chips, you would only roll 3 dice on your turn. Once a player is out of chips, (s)he is out of that game.

5. Play continues until one player has all the chips from the other players. The winner then also takes any chips that have accumulated in the cup. Winners must put 20% of their total winnings back into the cup for the next game. This is the winner's tax!

Variations

- Change the tax percentage on winnings, for example, 40%, 10%, 25%, etc.

- Conduct a *Pass It On* tournament.

Materials

Two standard dice.
One *Pizza Fractions Game* Board.
Two different colored pencils or pens.

Rules and Play

1. This is a comparing fractions game for 2 players or teams. The object of the game is to capture/eat the most pizzas.

2. Players/teams take turns rolling the cubes, forming fractions, and then coloring that fraction of a pizza on the game board with their color. The greater number on a cube is the number of parts into which a pizza on the game board has been cut and the lesser number shown on a cube is the number of parts to be covered. Players/teams may label several portions of different pizzas if they wish. If one is shown on both cubes, the player/team may only label the one whole pizza.

3. Play continues until all the pizzas are labeled. Then, a pizza is awarded to a player/team who has covered more than half of it. If each player/team has labeled half the pizza, neither player/team may claim it.

4. The player/team with the most pizzas wins.

Variation

- Change the requirement to win to obtain 4 pizzas in a row, column, or diagonal.

Pizza Fractions Game

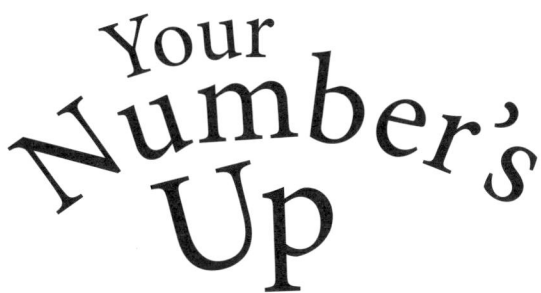

Your Number's Up

Materials

One deck of cards (point values: Aces = 1, Jokers = 0, Tens and Face Cards are removed).
One playing mat and record sheet for each player/team.
One set of instructions for each player/team (optional).

Preparation

Players decide if they want to play a high or low score wins game. Labels are then added to each place value mat so that the mats reflect the number of digits and the number of decimal places to be used in the game. For example, if the game involved five digits and two decimal places, then the place value mat would be labeled as shown below.

Hundreds	Tens	Ones	Tenths	Hundreths

Rules and Play

1. This is a place value and decision making game for 1-3 players/teams.

2. The object of the game is to build the largest or smallest number. The goal is determined by the players at the beginning of each game.

3. Play begins with the dealer placing a well-shuffled deck, face down, in the center between the players.

4. On each turn, players/teams select a card and location for the value of that card on their place value mat. Players/teams must select a different place on each turn.

5. Players/teams must name the place before they are allowed to put the drawn card in that location. For example, if a player drew a Seven and the game involved 3-digit numbers with 2 decimal places, (s)he would have to say, "I'm going to put the Seven in the ones place." Locations specified must be vacant and all placement decisions are final.

6. Play continues until all places are filled. When all places are filled, the winner is declared.

Variations

- Restrict the place value locations to ones and tens, or ones, tens, and hundreds.

- To make the standard game more challenging, expand the number of place value locations or play the game in other number bases. In base 5, the cards Ace through Four of each suit, plus the Jokers can be used.

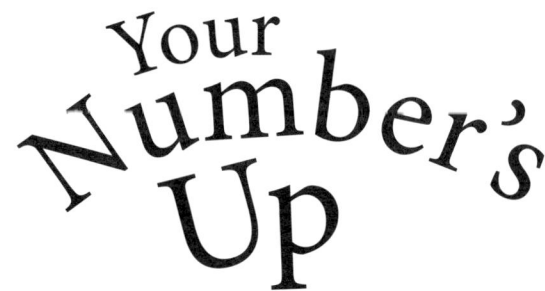

Pack

Goal: High or Low

Names	Places				

Goal: High or Low

Names	Places				

Materials

One playing board for each pair of players/teams.
Two standard dice and place markers for each pair of players/teams.
Two different colored pens or pencils for each player/team.

Rules and Play

1. This is a dice game for 2 players/teams. The object of the game is to get three marks in a row, column, or diagonal.

2. Players/teams take turns rolling the dice, one at a time, and plotting the point represented by the dice as shown below. Note that if a player/team rolls a 5 and a 3, (s)he may plot the ordered pair (5,3) or (3,5).

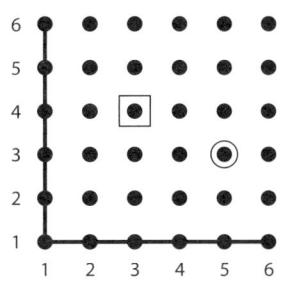

In this plotting whole numbers game, the first player rolled a 3 and 4 and the second player rolled a 5 and 3.

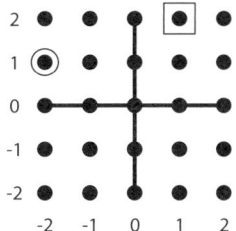

In this plotting integers game, the first player rolled a 1 and 2 and the second player rolled a -2 and 1. Both custom dice were labeled -1, -1. 0, 1, 2, -2.

Variations

- Use a larger grid and require that 4 or 5 marks in a row, column, or diagonal are needed to win.

- Allow 3 or 4 players/teams to play on the same grid.

POWER PLAY

Materials

Two standard or custom dice (an example is shown below).
One calculator and record sheet for each player/team.

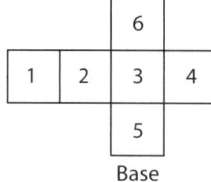
Base

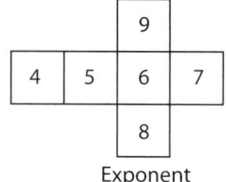
Exponent

Rules and Play

1. This is a game for 2-4 players or teams. Players/teams take turns rolling the dice and computing the result. For example, if a 3 and a 4 were rolled, the result would be $3^4 = 81$.

2. After computing the result, the score is recorded and the dice pass to the next player/team. After 8 rounds have been completed, total all the scores for each player/team. The largest total wins.

Variations

- Allow players/teams to use either die as the base and exponent.

- Change the goal to smallest total score wins.

- Play the game without a calculator. You may wish to make the problems easier by relabeling the dice as shown below.

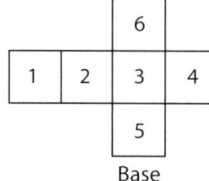
Base

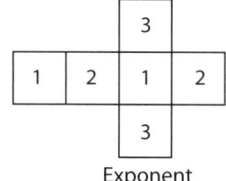
Exponent

- Use zero as an exponent.

- Allow the use of decimal bases.

- Adjust the exponent die to include negative integers.

- Adjust the base and exponent dice to include decimals and fractions.

Materials

Two custom dice for each player/team.
One metric ruler and a set of base-10 blocks for each player/team.

Rules and Play

1. This is a game for 2-4 players. The object of the game is to be the first player to construct a cubic decimeter. Note that $1 \text{ dm}^3 = 1000 \text{ cm}^3$.

2. To start the game, each player rolls the dice. The player with the highest total starts the play.

3. Players take turns tossing the dice and then selecting the blocks matching the roll. The example shows a sample roll and the layout for a custom made pair of dice. With this roll a player may select any combination totaling twenty-three cubic centimeters.

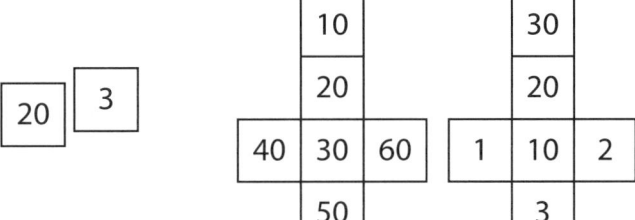

4. Players continue rolling the dice and building their cubic decimeter. The first player to complete the task is the winner.

5. If doubles are tossed (for example, 10,10; 20,20; 30,30), the player retains the dice and receives another turn. If a player rolls three doubles in a row, (s)he must remove 100 cubic centimeters from his/her cube.

Variations

- Change the dimensions of the solid that must be built.

- Change the numbers on the dice.

- Play *Block Buster*. In this game players start with a cubic decimeter block and go from 1000 cm^3 to 0 using subtraction.

Name The Number, Fraction or Shape

Objective

To provide practice in basic number facts, identification of polygons, and the meaning of fractions.

Materials

One die for each player.
One place marker for each player.
One *Name The Number, Fraction, and Shape* record sheet for each group.

Directions

1. This is a dice game for 1-5 players.

2. There are three separate activities. The object of each game is to move a place marker from the starting point to the halfway point and back again.

    Name That Number involves basic facts practice.
    Name That Shape involves identifying simple polygons.
    Name That Fraction involves the meaning of fractions.

3. Players take turns rolling the die. The roll of the die determines the number of squares a player may move. To move a place marker each player must solve the problem or answer the question in the square.

4. Only one place marker may occupy a square. If two players or teams land on the same square, the last player to arrive stays and the other player must return to the starting position.

5. The winner is the first player to return exactly to the starting position.

Variations

- Sample boards and one generic game board are provided on the following pages.

- To adapt the game to other units, change the problems on the board to suit the objectives. For example, problems involving operations with fractions, decimals, percent, solving proportions, solving equations, etc.

Name The Number

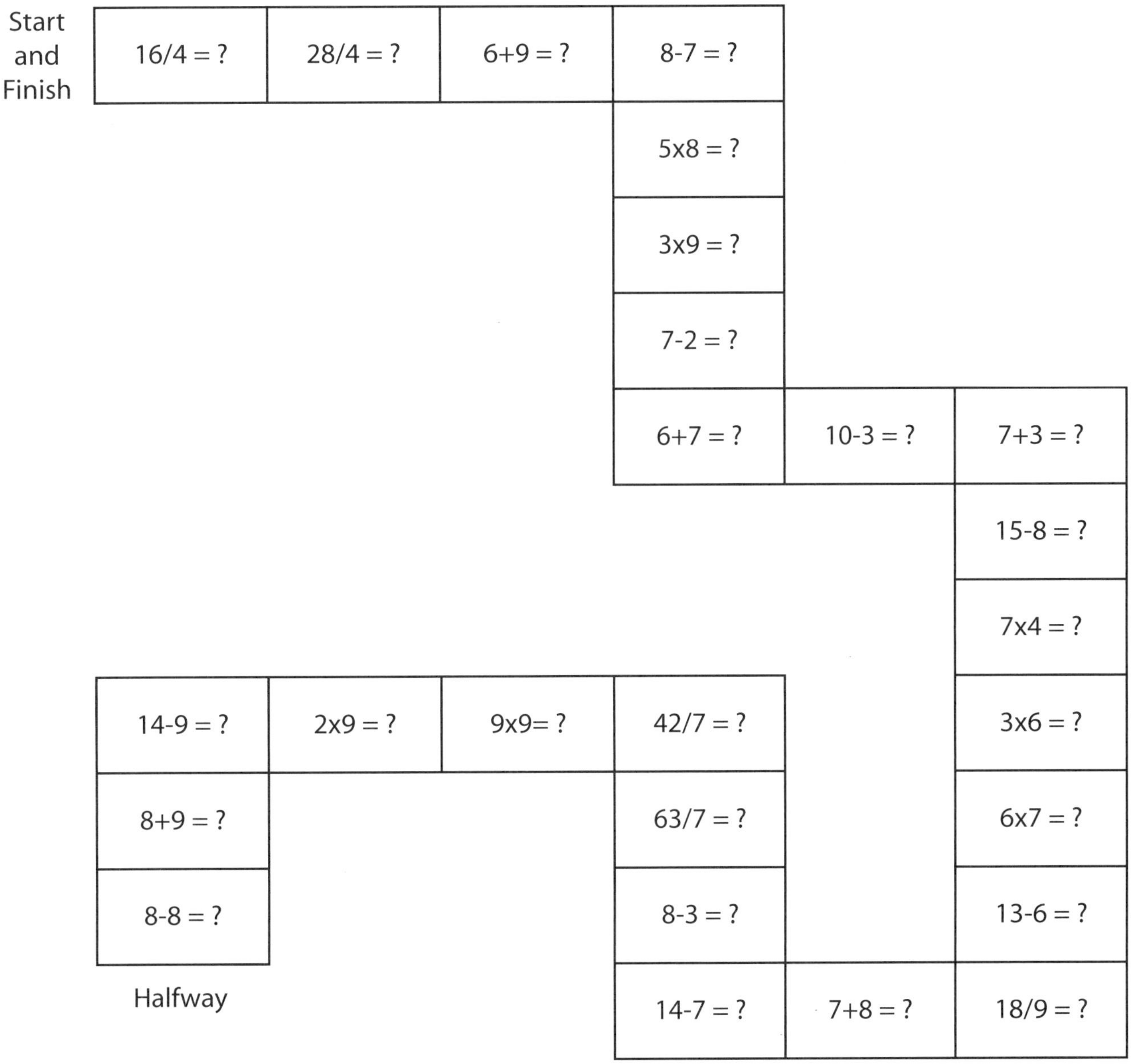

Start and Finish	16/4 = ?	28/4 = ?	6+9 = ?	8-7 = ?
				5x8 = ?
				3x9 = ?
				7-2 = ?
			6+7 = ?	10-3 = ?	7+3 = ?

(board continues)

- 15-8 = ?
- 7x4 = ?
- 3x6 = ?
- 6x7 = ?
- 13-6 = ?
- 18/9 = ?
- 7+8 = ?
- 14-7 = ?
- 8-3 = ?
- 63/7 = ?
- 42/7 = ?
- 9x9 = ?
- 2x9 = ?
- 14-9 = ?
- 8+9 = ?
- 8-8 = ?

Halfway

Math Games and Activities with Dice
© IPMG Publishing

47

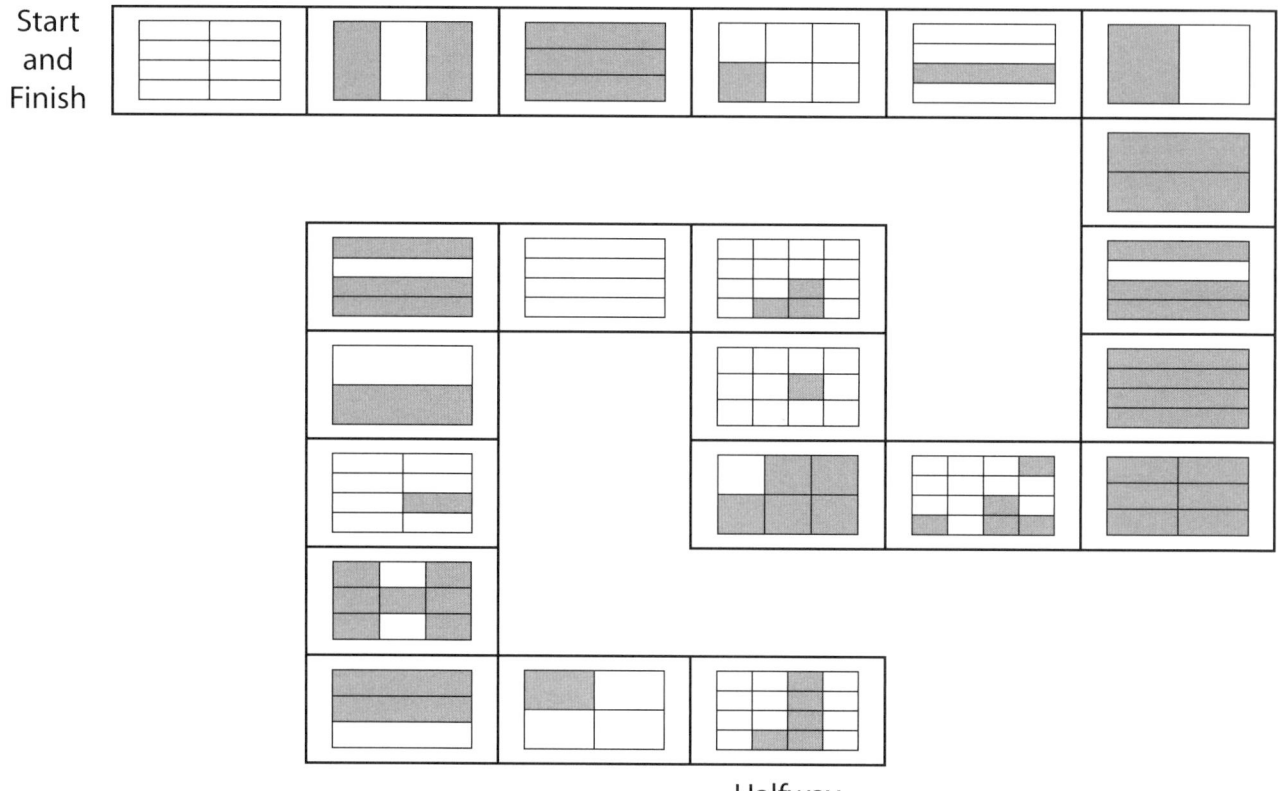

Name The Shape

Start and Finish

Halfway

Math Games and Activities with Dice
© IPMG Publishing

iplaymathgames.com

Name The Number, Fraction, and Shape

Start and Finish

Halfway

Materials

A meter stick.
A deck of cards.
A set of Cuisenaire rods.

Rules and Play

1. This is a game for 2 players/teams. The object of the game is to be the first player to construct a train exactly 100 centimeters long. If you do not have a set of Cuisenaire rods, you may play the game using a place marker to locate spots along the meter stick.

2. To start the game, each player draws a card. The player/team with the highest card starts the play.

3. Players/teams take turns drawing a card and then selecting the rods that are the correct length. For example, if a player drew a Five, (s)he would select a yellow rod because it is 5 cm in length. The rods are placed in a straight line (like a train) along the side of the meter stick. If a player/team draws a One-Eyed Jack, (s)he places a combination of rods whose total length is 11 cm and is given another turn. If a player/team draws a Joker, (s)he must remove 10 cm from his/her train.

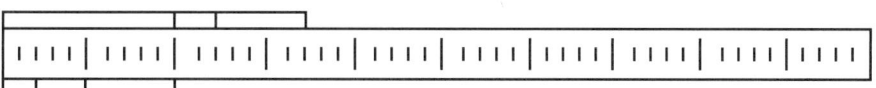

Variations

- Change the length of the winning train. (e.g. 50 cm, 2 m, etc.).

- Change the number of cards drawn.

- Play from 100 cm. to 0 using subtraction.

Rules and Play

3 standard dice.
One *It's Your Call* answer sheet.

Rules and Play

In this activity you will play a series of 30 games. Follow the procedures step by step and answer the questions.

First, player 1 names his/her number. His/her number is one of the numbers 1 through 6 that appear on a die.

Next, player 2 rolls three dice. Winnings are decided as follows:

    If the number DOES show up, player 2 pays player 1 $1 for each occurrence.
    If the number DOES NOT show up, player 1 pays $1 to player 2.

Play 30 games. Record the results in the table and see who wins.

Questions:

1. Did Player 1 win or lose, and how much?

2. For a single roll of the dice, the expected earnings, rounded to the nearest tenth of a cent, for player 1 is $.125. In a set of thirty games, how much would Player 1 be expected to win?

3. A player is considered lucky if (s)he wins more than expected and unlucky if (s)he wins less. Is Player 1 lucky or unlucky?

Extra Credit: Calculate the expected earnings per game of *It's Your Call* to the nearest tenth of a cent.

			Amount Won or Lost	
Round	Number Called	Numbers Rolled	Player 1	Player 2
1				
2				
3				
4				
5				
6				
7				
8				
9				
10				
11				
12				
13				
14				
15				
16				
17				
18				
19				
20				
21				
22				
23				
24				
25				
26				
27				
28				
29				
30				
		Final Total		

Materials

Three dice.

Rules and Play

The object of the game is to get a 6, 5, and 4 on three rolls of the dice. Players compete against the house. Each player gets 3 rolls. For example, if a player rolled a 3, 4, 1 on the first toss the player would hold the 4 and roll two dice on the second toss. If the results were 5, 2 on the second toss the player would hold the 5 and roll the one die on the third toss. If the result is 6 the player wins. If the result is any other number, the player loses.

1. Play at least 20 games of 6, 5, 4. Tally the number of wins and losses. Then answer the questions below.

   a. Mathematicians define a fair game of chance as one that gives all players/teams the same opportunity to win. Is this a fair game? Explain.

   b. If you owned a restaurant, would it be "good" to play this game with your customers for free food or beverages as a promotional scheme? Explain.

Are dice games fair? In this activity we use mathematics to make statements about prospects of wining or losing.
In *3 Ways to Win*, an ordinary die is used for this game. The "house" requires a player to pay $.50 each time a die is rolled.

The payoff to the player is summarized below.

    A multiple of 5, pays $1.00
    A multiple of 4, pays $.30
    A multiple of 3, pays $.20
    If the result is any other number, the player loses.

1. Let's play and analyze this game using a die

    a. Do this investigation. Roll one die 60 times. Record the result of each roll then find the frequency of each outcome.

    b. How much would you have won/lost if you had played this game at a casino?

2. Now we are ready to logically analyze *3 Ways to Win*. Use the results for the 60 games you recorded in exercise 1a. to help answer the following questions.

    a. What will it cost for 60 rolls of the dice?

    b. What are the total winnings you can expect from the 60 rolls of the dice?

Result	Frequency	Payoff	Total Payoff (60 games)
1			
2			
3			
4			
5			
6			
		Sum	

3. Complete the following logical analysis table of that *3 Ways to Win* using probability. Then use the table to answer the questions that follow. The first entry has been done for you.

Outcome	Probability	Payoff	Expected Payoff (60 games)
1	1/6	$0.00	1/6 x $0.00 x 60 = 0
2			
3			
4			
5			
6			
		Sum	

    a. What is the sum of the expected payoff column for 60 games?

    b. How much would it cost to play the 60 games?

    c. What is the gain or loss for 60 games?

    d. What is the average gain/loss per game?

    e. If we define the expected value of a game as the average per game result, what is the expected value of this game?

    f. Is this game fair? Explain.

4. Is it possible to make *3 Ways to Win* fair and keep the payoff scheme the same? Explain.

In this activity we use probability and statistics to analyze a two dice game.

Two Dice Sums is a game that is played using two ordinary dice. The person or gambling establishment running the game is often called the "house." In this game the house charges the player $1.00 each time the pair of dice are rolled. The outcome is the sum of the numbers showing when the dice are face up. The payoff to the player for each outcome is as follows.

    A total of 11 pays $10.00
    A total of 7 pays $1.00
    A total of 5 pays $0.50
    If the result is any other number, the player loses.

1. Play 72 games of *Two Dice Sums*. Tally each result and complete the table. Then answer the questions that follow.

Dice Sum	Tally	Frequency	Single Roll Payoff	Total Payoff
2				
3				
4				
5				
6				
7				
8				
9				
10				
11				
12				
			Total	

    a. If you played this game in a casino, how much would it cost for 72 rolls of the dice?

    b. Based on your results, what is the total amount won from the 72 rolls of the dice?

    c. What is your average per game gain or loss after 72 rolls?

Two Dice Sums

2. Complete the following chart using your knowledge of probability. Then answer the questions that follow. The first problem has been completed for you. Hint: Recall that there are 36 ways two dice can roll.

Dice Sum	Probability	Single Roll Payoff	Expected Payoff for 1 Game	Expected Payoff for 72 Games
2	1/36	0	0	0
3		0		
4		0		
5		$.50		
6		0		
7		$1.00		
8		0		
9		0		
10		0		
11		$10.00		
12		0		
		Total		

    a. What is the total payoff for 72 games?

    b. What is the total cost for 72 games?

    c. What is the gain or loss after 72 games?

3. Mathematicians define a fair game as one that gives all participants an equal chance to win. Is *Two Dice Sums* a fair game?

4. Ed said he could change the game *Two Dice Sums* so that it was fair and still keep the payoff the same. Is he correct? Explain.

6. What is the expected value of a fair game?

Math Games and Activities with Dice
© IPMG Publishing

Dice Calendar Puzzle

Instructions

Sharon wants to create a desk calendar using dice. She knows she needs to use the numbers from 0-9 on each die in order to represent all the days in each month of the year using both dice, but she is not sure how to do it. Help solve the problem. Label your answer on the dice patterns below. (Hint. Numbers may be reused.)

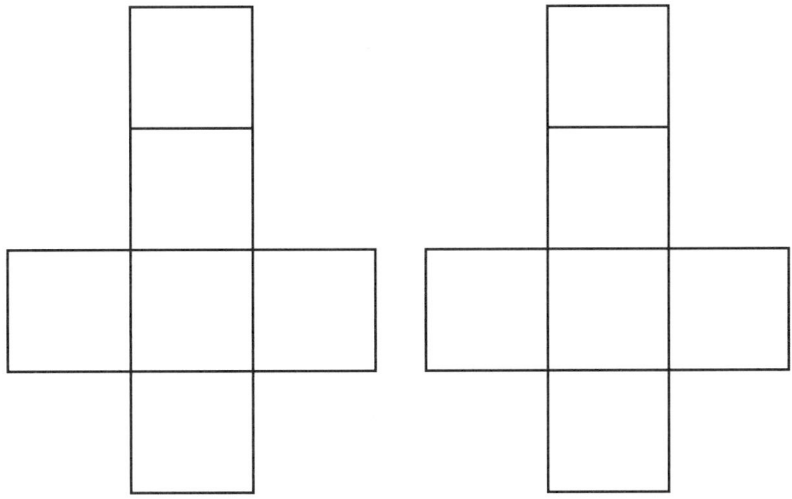

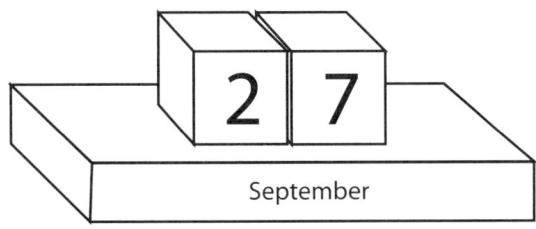

September

Stacking Dice Puzzles

1. What are the numbers and their positions that are not shown on the ordinary die below?

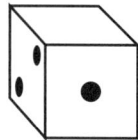

2. What is the sum of the numbers shown on opposite faces of an ordinary die?

3. What is the sum of all the dots on one die?

4. What is the sum of all the dots on two, three, four, and five dice?

5. What is the sum of all the dots on ten dice, one hundred dice, one thousand dice?

6. What is the sum of all the dots on n dice?

7. Make a stack of two dice so that the sum of each side of the stack is the same. Is it possible? If so, what is the sum of each side?

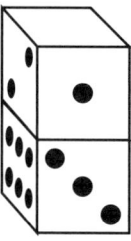

8. Make a stack of three dice so the sum of each side of the stack is the same. Is it possible? If so, what is the sum of each side?

Stacking Dice Puzzles

9. Make a stack of four dice so the sum of each side of the stack is the same. Is it possible? If so, what is the sum of each side?

10. Examine your answers to problems 7-9. Put your results in a table and look for patterns. Then predict the result for using 6 and 7 dice.

Number of Dice in Stack	Sum of Each Side of Stack
2	
3	
4	
5	
6	
7	

11. Tammy said, "Here are the results I found for stacking an even number of dice."

Number of Dice in Stack	2	4	6	8
Sum of Each Side of Stack	7	14	21	28

    a. Is she correct?

    b. What is the sum of each side of a stack of 12 dice?

    c. What is the sum of each side of a stack of 100 dice?

    d. What is the sum of each side of a stack of 1000 dice?

    e. What is the sum of each side of a stack of n dice?

12. Make up your own stacking dice puzzle.

1. What are the numbers and their positions that are not shown on the ordinary die below?

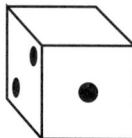

2. What is the sum of the numbers shown on opposite faces of an ordinary die?

3. Here is a stack of two dice.

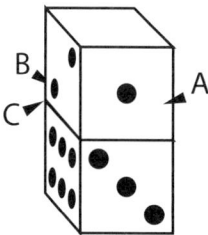

    a. What is the sum of the dots on the two faces of side A?

    b. What is the sum of the dots on the two faces of side B?

    c. What is the sum of the dots on the two touching faces?

4. Here is a stack of three dice.

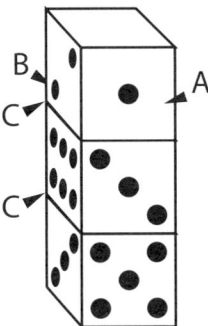

   a. What is the sum of the dots on the three faces of side A?

   b. What is the sum of the dots on the three faces of side B?

   c. What is the sum of the dots on the four touching faces?

5. Here is a stack of four dice.

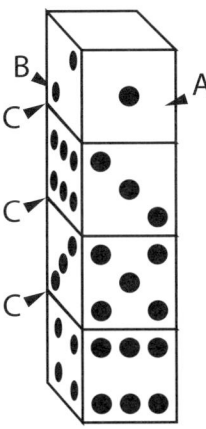

   a. What is the sum of the dots on the four faces of side A?

   b. What is the sum of the dots on the four faces of side B?

   c. What is the sum of the dots on the six touching faces?

6. Examine your answers to problems 3-5. What patterns do you notice?

7. Make up your own touching dice puzzle.

Rolling 3 Dice Trick

1. Work with a partner to try the trick outlined below.

    Step 1: While your back is turned, have your partner take out 3 ordinary dice.

    Step 2: Have your partner roll the dice and secretly add the values shown on the faces. For example, (s)he might roll a 5, 6, 1 and get a total of 12.

    Step 3: Have your partner pick up any one of the 3 dice (s)he rolled and secretly add the number on the bottom to the previous total. For example, in Step 2 a player might select the 5. The number opposite the 5 would be a 2. So, the new total would be 14.

    Step 4: Have your partner roll the same die again and secretly add the result shown to the previous total. For example, if the player rolled again and got a 6, the new total would be 20.

    Step 5: Turn around and add 7 to what you see on the die faces to predict the secret total obtained by your partner. In the example, the faces showing would be 6, 1, 6. Adding 7 to 13 gives you 20!

2. Explain why this trick works using algebra. Hint. Let the letters a, b, and c represent the values shown on the dice. Also note that opposite faces on an ordinary die always add to 7, so the number on the opposite face "a" is $7 - a$, the number on the opposite face "b" is $7 - b$ and the number on the opposite face "c" is $7 - c$.

3. Make up a new dice trick.

Touching Faces Dice Trick

1. Try the trick outlined below.

    Step 1: Stack three dice on top of the other. An example is shown.

    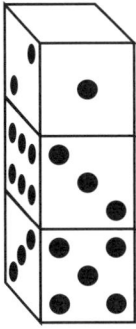

    Step 2: Look at the top two dice. Add the values shown on the two faces that touch each other. Record the answer.

    Step 3: Look at the bottom two dice. Add the values shown on the two faces that touch each other. Then add the answer to the sum you found in Step 2. Record the answers.

    Step 4: Add the value shown on the bottom face of the bottom die to the sum you found in Step 3. Record the result.

    Step 5: Subtract the value shown on the top face of the top die from 21. The answer is the final sum.

2. Explain why this trick works using algebra. Hint. Let the letters a and b represent the top and bottom faces of the bottom die; c and d the top and bottom faces of the middle die; e and f, the top and bottom faces of the top die.

    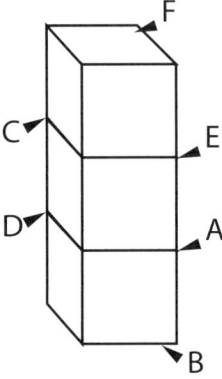

3. Make up a new 3 stacked dice trick based on your algebraic analysis in problem 2.

Standard Cube Dice Template

Make a copy of this page. Then duplicate the desired number of copies on thick paper or tagboard. Finally, cut on the solid lines and fold on the dotted lines and tape the edges together. You may also use the tabs on the sides to glue the sides together.

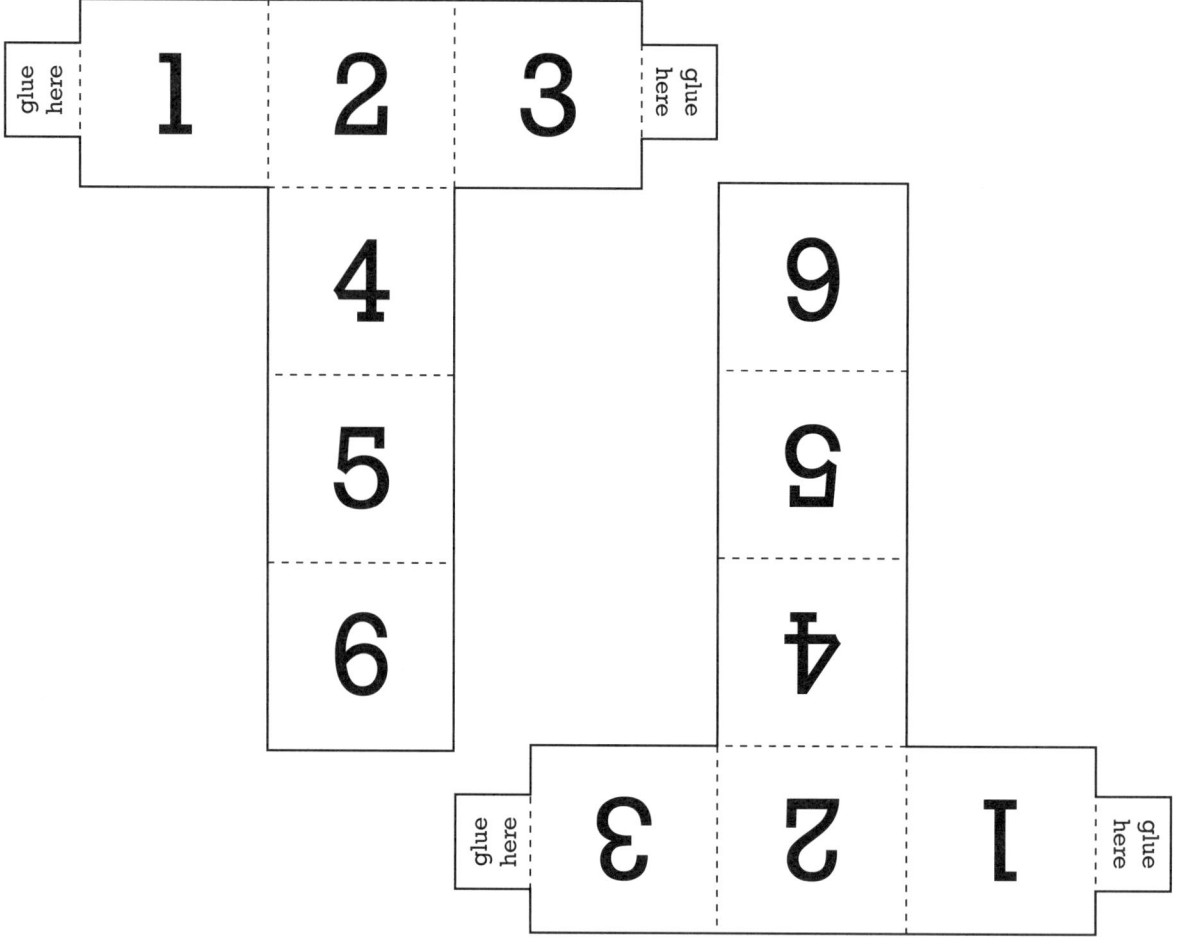

Math Games and Activities with Dice
© IPMG Publishing

Octahedral Dice Template

Make a copy of this page. Then duplicate the desired number of copies on thick paper or tagboard. Finally, cut on the solid lines and fold on the dotted lines and tape the edges together. You may also use the tabs on the sides to glue the sides together.

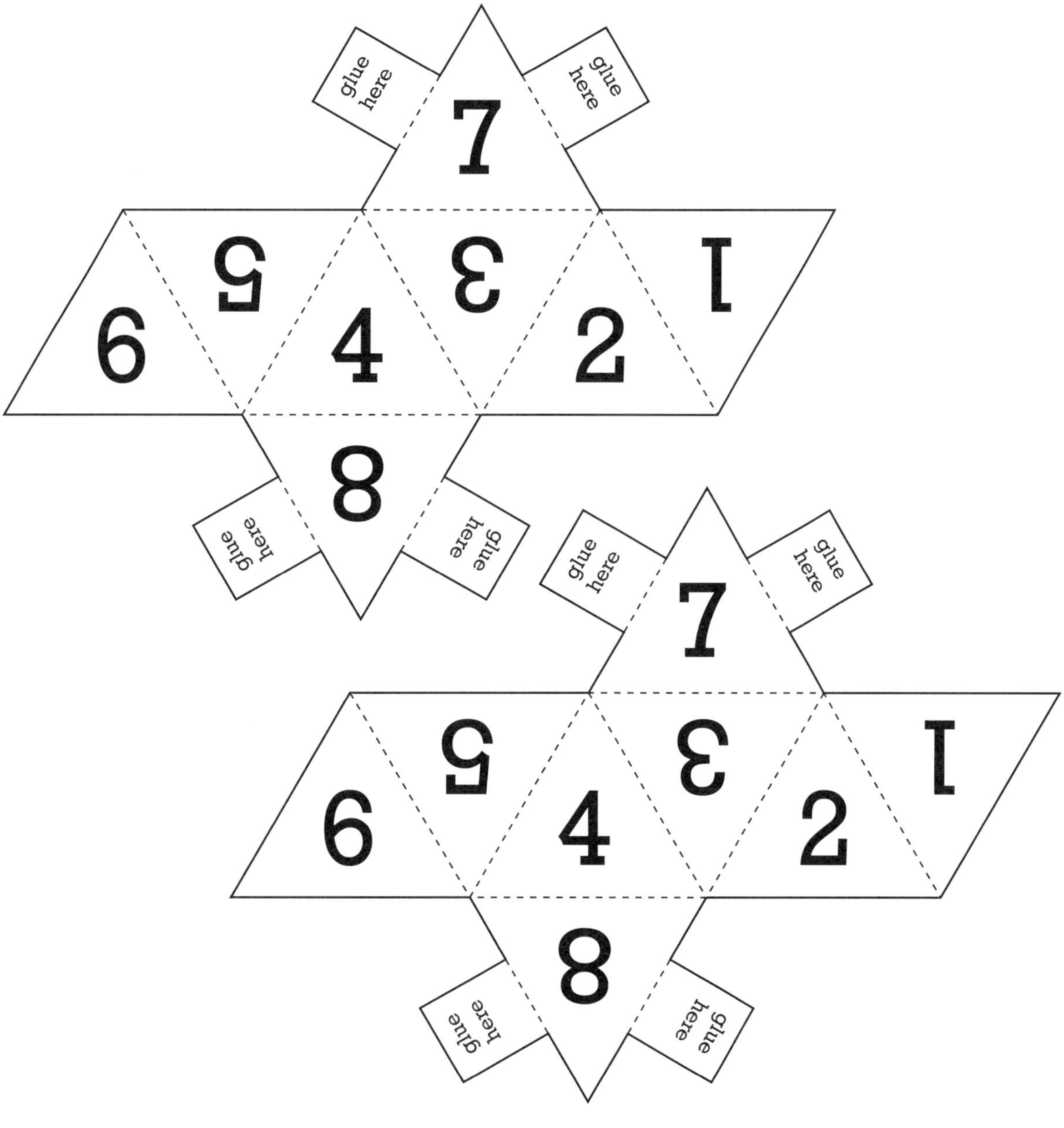

Math Games and Activities with Dice
© IPMG Publishing

Dodecahedron Dice Template

Make a copy of this page. Then duplicate the desired number of copies on thick paper or tagboard. Finally, cut on the solid lines and fold on the dotted lines and tape the edges together.

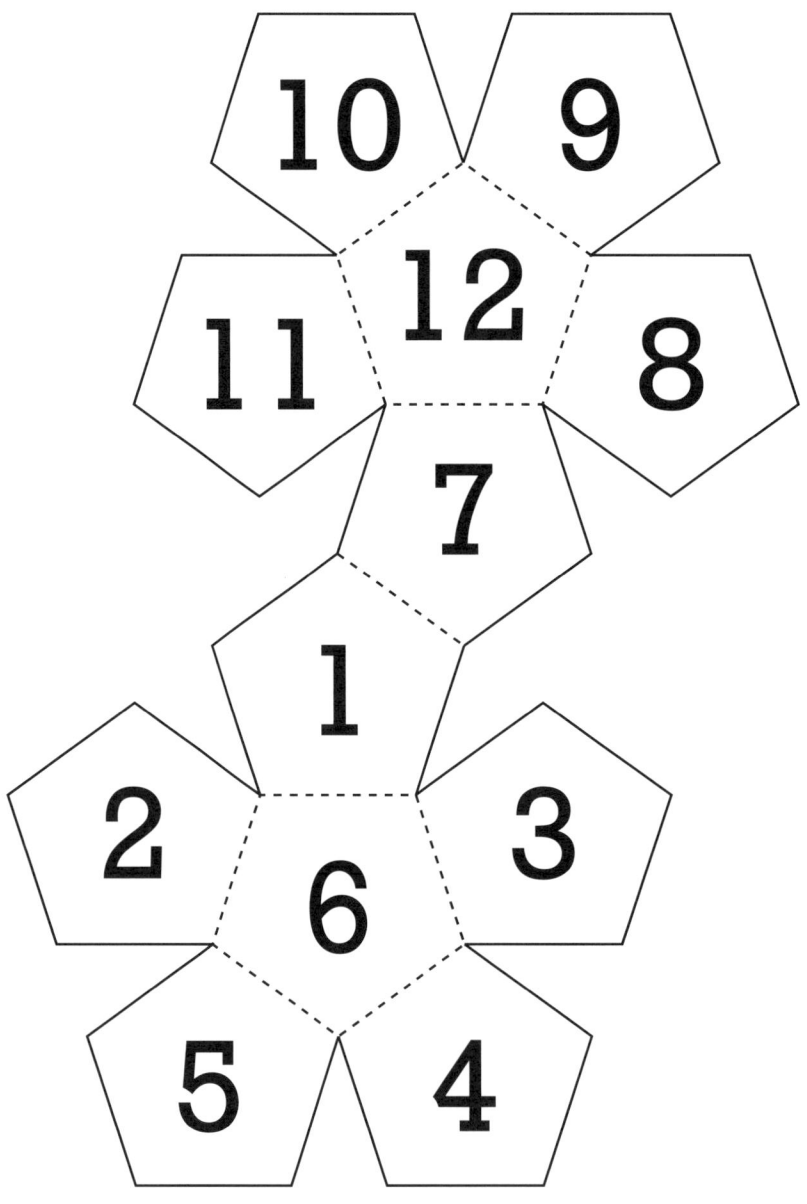

Selected Answers and Comments

Page 44: Power Play. Suggested follow up questions are provided below.

1. What is the largest score possible in one round of a game of Power Play if two ordinary dice are used? Answer: $6^6 = 46{,}656$.
2. What is the smallest score possible in one round of a game of Power Play if two ordinary dice are used? Answer: One to any power (e.g. $1^6 = 1$).
3. What is the second largest score possible in one round of a game of Power Play if two ordinary dice are used? Answer: $5^6 = 15{,}625$.
4. What is the second smallest score possible in one round of a game of Power Play if two ordinary dice are used? Answer: $2^1 = 2$.
5. What is the highest total score possible in an eight-round game of Power Play using two ordinary dice? Answer: $46{,}656 \times 8 = 373{,}248$.

Page 45: Block Builder. 2a. 10 2b. 100 2c. 10 2d. 100 2e. 100 2f. 10 To save time and encourage cooperation, consider having pairs of students work together to build a cubic decimeter. Have each group tally the number of turns needed to complete the task. Also, consider awarding a small prize to the group who completes the job in the fewest number of turns.

What is the average number of turns needed to complete a game in our class?

What is the minimum number of turns needed to build a cubic decimeter using a die labeled 0, 5, 10, 25, 50, 100? Answer: 10

What is the maximum number of turns needed to build a cubic decimeter using a die labeled 0, 5, 10, 25, 50, 100? Answer: Infinite

What is the theoretical average number of rolls that should be needed to build a cubic decimeter using a die labeled 0, 5, 10, 25, 50, 100?
Answer: $[5 + 10 + 25 + 50 + 100] / 6 \approx 31.67$, $1000/31.67 \approx 31.58$, so, 32 turns.

Similar questions can be posed using ordinary dice.

Page 51: One Meter Dash. To save time and encourage cooperation, consider having pairs of students work together to build a cubic decimeter. Have each group tally the number of turns needed to complete the task. Also, consider awarding a small prize to the group who completes the job in the fewest number of turns.

What is the average number of turns needed to complete a game in our class?

What is the minimum number of turns needed to build a cubic decimeter using a die labeled 0, 2, 10, 1, 5, -1? Answer: 10

What is the maximum number of turns needed to build a cubic decimeter using a die labeled 0, 2, 10, 1, 5, -1? Answer: Infinite

What is the theoretical average number of rolls that should be needed to build a cubic decimeter using a die labeled 0, 2, 10, 1, 5, -1?
Answer: $[0 + 2 + 10 + 1 + 5 + -1] / 6 \approx 2.83$, $100/2.83 = 35.34$, so, 36 turns.

Similar questions can be posed using ordinary dice.

Page 52-53: It's Your Call. 2. $.125 \times 30 = \$3.75$ 3. Lucky. Extra Credit: The expected earnings for this game can be calculated as outlined below. Note: The probability of one five on each of the dice is 1/6. So, the probability of getting one five on the 3 dice is:

First Die 5	Second Die not 5	Third Die not 5	
1/6	5/6	5/6	= 25/216
First Die not 5	Second Die 5	Third Die not 5	
5/6	1/6	5/6	= 25/216
First Die not 5	Second Die not 5	Third Die 5	
5/6	5/6	1/6	= 25/216

The probability of one five on the three dice is…75/216

Selected Answers and Comments

First Die 5	Second Die 5	Third Die not 5	
1/6	1/6	5/6	= 5/216
First Die 5	Second Die not 5	Third Die 5	
1/6	5/6	1/6	= 5/216
First Die not 5	Second Die 5	Third Die 5	
5/6	1/6	1/6	= 5/216

The probability of not getting two fives on the three dice is...15/216

The probability of three fives on the 3 dice is:
1/6 x 1/6 x 5/6 = 1/216.

So, the expected earnings for Player 1 are:
75/216($1) + 15/216($2) + 1/216($3) = 96/216 or .44

The expected earnings for Player 2 are:
31/216(-1) = -31/216 = -.1435 or -.14

Page 60: 654. Sample results from 3 sets of 20 games are provided.

W	L	W	L	W	L
|||	‖‖‖ ‖‖‖	‖‖‖	‖‖‖ ||||	‖‖‖
	‖‖‖ ||	‖‖‖		‖‖‖
	‖‖‖	‖‖‖		‖‖‖

1a. No. Explanations will vary. 1b. Yes. Explanations will vary.

Pages 55-56: 3 Ways to Win. 2a. $30. 2b. Answers will vary. An example is shown.

Result	Frequency	Payoff	Total
1	11	0	0
2	5	0	0
3	12	.20	2.40
4	13	.30	3.90
5	11	1	11
6	8	.20	1.60

Sum: 18.70

3e. $E = 1(\frac{1}{6}) + .30(\frac{1}{6}) + .20(\frac{2}{6})$

$$E = \frac{1+.3+.4}{6} = \frac{1.7}{6} \approx .28\overline{3}$$

3f. No. The expected payoff for a fair game is zero. In this game it is .283 - .50 is approximately equal to -.22
4. Yes. Charge less to game play. .283 is the expected value, so charging .28 would be close.

Pages 57-58: Two Dice Sums. 1a. $72 2a. $54 2b. $72 2c. -$22 3. No 4. Yes. Change the cost of playing. 56/72 = .78. If we find the product of each outcome and the probability of that outcome and add the results, we get

$$[(\tfrac{2}{36}) \times 10] + [1 \times (\tfrac{2}{36})] + [(\tfrac{1}{2}) \times (\tfrac{14}{36})] = (\tfrac{28}{36}) \approx .78$$

5. $E = [\tfrac{4}{36}(0) + \tfrac{3}{36}(0) + \tfrac{2}{36}(0) + \tfrac{1}{36}(0)] - \tfrac{1}{(1)} = \tfrac{28}{36} - 1 =$

$\tfrac{7}{9} - 1 = \tfrac{-2}{9}$ or $-.\overline{2}$

Page 59: Dice Calendar Puzzle. Answers will vary. One example is shown here. Note that the numerals 6 and 9 are shown by rotating the cube.

		5				6	
0	1	2	3	1	2	0	7
		4				8	

Selected Answers and Comments

Page 60: Stacking Dice Puzzles 1. 1,6 2,5 3,4 2. 7 3. 21 4. 42, 63, 84, 105 5. 210, 21000, 21000 6. 21n 7. Yes. 7 8. No. 9. Yes. 21 10.

Number of Dice in Stack	Sum of Each Side of Stack
2	7
3	Impossible
4	14
5	Impossible
6	21
7	Impossible

11a. Yes. 11b. 42 11c. 350 11d. 3500 11e. n/2 x 7

Page 62-63: Touching Faces Dice Puzzles. 1. Top face is a 4. Bottom face is a 3. Left face is a 6. Right face is a 5. 2a. 5+1=6. 2b. 6+4=10 2c. (3+2)=5 3a. 5+1+4=10 3b. 6+4+2=12 3c. (3+2) + (5+1) = 11 4a. 5+1+4+3=13 4b. 6+4+2+1=13 4c. (3+2) + (5+1) + (2+6) = 19 5. The key to solving each problem is knowing that the sum of the opposite faces on an ordinary die is 7.

Page 64: Rolling 3 Dice Trick. Let a, b, and c represent the values shown on the dice. Adding the numbers on the facts can be represented by: a + b + c.

One die is picked up and the number on the bottom face of that die is added to the previous sum. So, the number on the opposite face of a is 7-a, the number on the opposite face of b is 7-b, and the number on the opposite side of c is 7-c.

Suppose "b" is the number shown on the die picked up. Since the number on the opposite face of b is 7-b, the new total will be (a+b+c) + (7-b). Simplifying we get a+c+7 as the new total.

Since all three dice have the same characteristic number arrangement, the new sum will always be equal to 7 plus the values on the two dice not selected.

Rolling the selected die again gives another number to add to our total. Let's call it d. Note that d might have the same value as a, b, or c, but it doesn't matter. Adding the value d to running total we get: a+c+7+d.

What you see on the table is a+c+d.

What your partner has totaled is a+c+d+7.

All you need to do is add 7 to what you see to predict your partner's secret total.

Teacher comment: Using stickers labeled a, b, c, and d on the 3 dice can be useful in explaining the proof to students.

Page 65: Touching Faces Dice Trick.

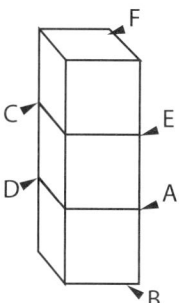

2.

Proof.

Recall that the sum of opposite faces of a die = 7. So, we know that (a+b)=7, (c+d)=7, and (e+f)=7. We also know that (a+b) + (c+d) + (e+f) = 21.

What we need to show is that (e+c) + (d+a) + b =21 – f is another way to write (a+b) + (c+d) + (e+f) = 21.

We can do this by starting with (a+b) + (c+d) + (e+f) = 21. Then, removing the parentheses we get a + b + c + d + e + f = 21. Next we change the order of the variables and get e + c + d + a + b + f = 21. Finally, we subtract f from both sides of the equation and get e + c + d + a + b = 21 – f. So, it will work all the time!

Teacher comment: Using stickers labeled a, b, c, d, e, and f on the 3 dice can be useful in explaining proof to students.

Notes